A GLIMPSE OF THE ANCIENT SUNLIGHT

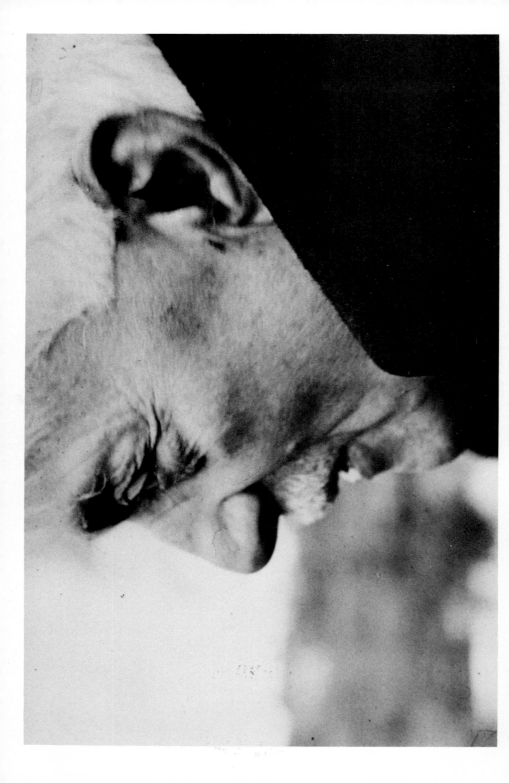

SUE CARON

A GLIMPSE
OF THE
ANCIENT SUNLIGHT

Memories of Henry Williamson

With a Foreword & Notes by
BROCARD SEWELL

First published 1986 by
The Aylesford Press

A GLIMPSE OF THE ANCIENT SUNLIGHT
Copyright © Sue Caron 1986

Foreword & Notes Copyright © Brocard Sewell 1986
Illustrations Copyright © Oswald Jones 1986

Standard edition 1 869955 00 5
Signed edition 1 869955 01 3

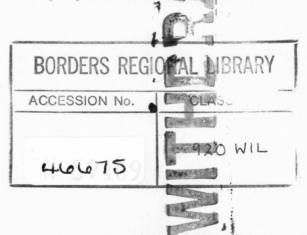
Printed and Bound in Great Britain
SMITH SETTLE
Otley, West Yorkshire

CONTENTS

Page

FOREWORD 9

A GLIMPSE OF THE ANCIENT SUNLIGHT 13

NOTES 33

ILLUSTRATIONS

Henry Williamson   *Frontispiece*

Henry at Aylesford Priory   *Facing page* 13

FOREWORD

HENRY WILLIAMSON'S biography is being written
by his son Richard, but there is so much biographical ma-
terial to be sifted through that probably we shall not see this
book for some years. We are likely to see rather sooner Dr
Wheatley Blench's critical study of Henry Williamson's
writings, which is now nearing completion. In the mean
time we have the volume of essays critical and biographical,
Henry Williamson: The Man, The Writings, with an introduction by Ronald Duncan, published in 1980, and Daniel
Farson's memoir, *Henry: An Appreciation*, published in 1982.

Many shorter writings on Williamson have appeared in
magazines since his death in 1977, notably in the *Henry
Williamson Society Journal* and the *Durham University Journal*.
To these can now be added Sue Caron's memoir, a re-
working of an earlier writing that was published obscurely
in 1977 and has long been unobtainable.

Sue Caron's memoir is a work of love; that is what gives
it its special quality. The old adage says that Love is blind,
but the careful reader will see that this writer is not blind
at all; that she is not unaware of Henry Williamson's
'difficult' side. It would seem, though, that with her he was
able to transcend some of his limitations. But the relationship could probably not have become permanent.

Henry Williamson could do many things, and he did
them all well. And he could teach anyone willing to learn
how to do many things himself: how to prune an apple-
tree, how to build a fireplace, how to lay a fire so that it
would light immediately and keep alight, and how to
rebuild a faulty fireplace so that it would cease giving
out smoke. But for Henry there was only one way to do
anything, and that was the *right* way. It must always have
been difficult for any companion to live up to such an

exacting standard. Indeed, not only was this perfectionism at times a strain on the patience of Henry's friends and familiars: it was a strain on himself. He applied the same rigorous standard to his writing, so that he was rarely satisfied with it. It is to this remorseless striving for perfection that we owe his great works that are now part of the heritage of English literature.

Perhaps it is not really possible to teach anyone to write, but it is certainly possible to encourage them and to guide them. Henry was generous of such encouragement, not least when he was editing *The Adelphi*. Many of his discoveries and protégés have become successful and established writers. He discerned potential talent in Sue Caron, and I imagine it was circumstances rather than choice that led to her taking to photography rather than to writing as a means of livelihood.

She has a good memory, and a good ear for human speech, but she has found a valuable *aide-mémoire* in the letters that she received from Henry. I have often heard him talking about his *Ancient Sunlight* novels, during the years when he was writing them, in exactly the manner she has here recreated. This wonderful novel-sequence tells the story of Phillip Maddison, who is in some sense, although not a self-portrait, Henry Williamson's alter ego. It begins with the courtship and marriage of his parents, back in late Victorian days, and continues through the war of 1914–18 down to a little after the end of the Second World War. It is at once a panorama of our times, an analysis and exposure of the deeper causes of the decay and wreck of Europe and its civilization, and a spiritual testimony arising from one man's deeply-felt experience of all this. The fifteen novels in this series are not all of the same high excellence. That was not to be expected. The best, perhaps, are the magical first volume, *The Dark Lantern*, the early books covering Phillip's childhood and schooldays, and the five novels of the 1914–18 war years, which record Phillip's experiences as an officer of the British Army in France and Flanders; but the later volumes which deal in part with his farming experiences in East Anglia, and his battle to reclaim the

'Bad Lands', on which local pundits said that crops would never grow, are no less tense with excitement. Phillip's marriages and romantic attachments reflect something of Henry Williamson's own history, but as transmuted by the light of imagination.

Sue Caron's memoir brings before us vividly the tensions and mental agonies of Henry Williamson as he struggled with the creation of his extraordinary masterpiece, *A Chronicle of Ancient Sunlight*.

Henry Williamson was a generous, warm-hearted man. Sue Caron appears to have seen him almost uniformly at his best; and this says much for her. If her testimony brings new readers to the works of this great writer, that will be its chief vindication: if any vindication is needed.

BROCARD SEWELL

A GLIMPSE OF THE ANCIENT SUNLIGHT

Memories of Henry Williamson

'AND WHEN I hear her voice, I rejoice – I rejoice, and my heart sings with the lark.'

Lovers I have had many, real friends I have had few. Perhaps it was fate that I should meet Henry Williamson. I have never tried to plot out my own destiny, but when I was dreaming of being a writer Henry came into my life and left his mark.

I'd gone on one of my run-away jaunts, wanting only to escape from myself and the people who seemed so determined to become involved in my life. Down a quiet country lane somewhere in Devon I was wandering, when a tired Austin A40 with a registration plate HOD drew to a halt opposite me. I walked over and stared in at the driver.

He had a Byronic face which was heavily sun-tanned. Beautiful sculptured features and heavy lines of age and experience were carved into the tight-fitting flesh. I asked him if he was going to Ilfracombe; he said he was, and we set off.

After a few moments I recognized his face, for the *Sunday Times* had recently published a feature on him. I mentioned *The Star-Born*.[1] He giggled. 'Yes, I'm a writer. Williamson's the name.' We drove into a field, and bumped and ground our way across to an odd little hut on the other side.

He made me some fresh orange-juice, and we sat on the grass outside the hut, his tall gangling body spread across the ground like a young graduate. I was fascinated by his features, his crop of straight snowy white hair which continually fell across his face. His face was scourged by experience, by terror, and a beauty of life. He was, as I was soon to learn, a man who had been through the First

World War and who had lived all his life in unhappiness, never really finding an enduring love. But during that first meeting he seemed to have a wonderful sense of humour, and used long complicated words and made up silly rhymes that amused me. I felt warm towards him, as though I had known him all my life.

When he asked me if I would like to look round the hut, I felt I belonged there. There was row upon row of beautiful books, while his desk was a deluge of papers, for he was working on a new book. He explained how he wrote for long tedious hours, how he never stopped creating people, places, characters, and reliving his life through his pen.

In the corner of a windowsill on the first floor I noticed a small mother bee bathing in the sunlight. 'She'll be all right now. Poor creature, lost one of her wings. I've been feeding her on honey, flies, and spiders,' he said as his thin ghostly fingers pointed a tea-spoonful of honey at the bee, which wandered towards it as though she had been trained.

We sat for a long time by this windowsill, staring out at the sea and the strange desolate fields where he lived, wrote and, I imagined, loved. Between us there was an affinity that I'd never found with anyone else. I was young and seeking knowledge, rather like someone looking for a religious path on which to walk.

Late in the afternoon he gave me a lift to Ilfracombe, and said that he would show me his cottage in Capstone Place. He was obviously a local character. The cottage itself was chaotic, with papers, files, books in disarray throughout.

My feelings towards Henry Williamson and, indeed, our subsequent affair are among my most beautiful memories. I respected not only his understanding of human nature but also his love of all created nature, which was something we both shared. I think he was probably able to write with such feeling only because he himself felt as if he belonged amid the earth.

That first night he prepared pure vegetable soup for me. He believed in the good natural things in life, and perhaps *Dandelion Days* gives more insight into the author's life than any other book that he wrote. His pen can regurgitate history, but at the same time sprinkles personalities and character studies into the pages, thus bringing the epic alive. I am surprised that even now none of his books except *Tarka the Otter*[2] has been made into a film.

Love and Henry Williamson were worlds apart. His own early love story is recorded in *The Dream of Fair Women*.[3] He would often talk about this particular book, and as we came to know one another I realized that he was a passionate, warm creature who needed human contact, who like me needed love and affection to feel that he was alive. Sometimes he would hold me in his arms and squeeze me tightly to him, as though he never wanted to let me go.

I can remember those evenings we spent together in the hut, when he would pile logs onto the fire and we would sit with just the flickering flames lighting the room. How immortal he looked sitting there, his face illuminated by the flames, his soft thin pink lips curtained at the top by a white moustache. I found him very attractive sexually. He reminded me of a wild goose. No one would ever capture his spirit completely, though I visualized it skimming the lakes of humanity and dipping into the forests of nature in order to survive. He often talked about the wild geese which flew in from the sea; he explained, as only Henry Williamson could do, that they had their own flight path and that no one could ever deflect them from it. I imagined that his own life was rather similar to that of the wild goose. He knew that his purpose in life was to write, and he had the most amazing memory I had ever come across.

If my life suddenly came to an abrupt halt and I could look back on the times when I was happy I would choose to relive the moments I spent with him; those long evenings lying together in front of the fire, reading out chapters of his books, or going through his freshly-typed manuscripts.

I felt even in those days that it must have been a very similar scene to that of Scott Fitzgerald and Sheilah Graham, although I denied myself the pleasure of setting up home with Henry Williamson. But I did love to watch him work; he would sit anywhere, and, indeed, often in bed, writing Proust-like, and always joking about his work. He typed erratically, in bursts; and then he would stop and think, his eyes sometimes filling with tears, and I would know that he was reliving a particularly painful part of his life, or becoming so engrossed with his characters that he was living for them.

I loved to watch him sleep, his long lashes spiking the air, the lines on his face suddenly disappearing, his waxen hands gripping the sheet as though they were those of one of his soldier boys dying in some muddy trench on the Somme.

Yes, like Scott Fitzgerald with his Sheilah, he encouraged me to write. He would sit for hours explaining the technicalities of writing. He gave me a long list of books to read, and I grew during the months that followed to love and respect him. He offered me everything, and yet all he was really offering was himself. I had neither the strength nor the sense to take up his offer.

That first beautiful weekend together was followed by time spent in London, talking and learning about one another. We would drink at the Savage Club, and walk hand in hand along the Embankment, laughing and throwing stones into the Thames. He seemed to work very hard at being Henry Williamson, never ceasing to write, often into the early hours of the morning, until those tranquil blue eyes were tired and his white hair fell across his brow and he drifted into sleep. But his sleep was restless, as though he could find no real peace. Very often he would talk or moan gently like a baby gurgling in its cot. He would raise his hands in anger, and then suddenly all would be calm, as if some almighty tempest had swept across his brain. Sometimes, despite his huge frame, I would take him in my arms and hold him close, so close that our hearts would beat together. I wanted to block out with kisses and warmth the echo of the battlefield. I longed to annihilate the screams of soldiers dying on the Somme, which he always said he heard whenever he lay down to sleep.

In those days we lived a euphoric existence, planning travel together, studying nature. We explored one another in every way. His kiss was like that of a frightened animal, coming forward for food, his lips and nose gently sniffing danger in the air, then suddenly finding that the danger had passed and that I was there to comfort him. It was a torrid relationship. He spoke about marriage many times, but I was too young to appreciate his offer. He talked of my body as though it were Dresden china. He would often stroke me as if I were an animal he had not tamed.

Sometimes we would arrange to meet, but he would walk straight past me in the street, pretending that he didn't know me. The first time he did this, I thought he was ill. I ran up to him outside the Savage Club and grabbed his hand. He rushed off down the street, laughing and telling me that he was going to get a police-woman because I was attacking him. Then sometimes he would ring up and pretend to be an ambassador, or a famous film star.

I never knew what to expect from him. On one occasion, when we were out to dinner together, he called the waiter over when the bill arrived and asked if he could pay in rose petals. On another occasion we were walking down Charing Cross Road when he suddenly stopped, as if wires had jerked him to a halt. I wondered what was wrong with him. He turned and looked right at me, those blue eyes suddenly clouded with tears.

'Tell me you love me. Go on, shout it out as loud as you can. Tell me you love me, you love me,' he bellowed. People turned and looked at us as if we were crazy. Of course, in those days I was somewhat inhibited, and found it difficult to shout out anything, least of all what he wanted.

Yet, deep in my heart I had this ever-raging desire to make him happy. I have often thought since that if only the timing had been different I might have traced a path to Ilfracombe and stayed there with my own sweet Orion. As it was, I soon found myself typing his manuscripts.

Henry was a very generous man, although in his more depressed moods he would plead poverty and tell me he was down to his last shilling. I would often laugh at him, and sometimes grumble at him; but I was always tremendously moved when he talked about the 1914–1918 war. I think perhaps I was as interested in it as he was, and since I was crazy about Rupert Brooke we would often spend hours just talking about people he had known in those days. He had a few good friends, both young and old, and he would often recall them to me. Some were young beautiful people: sallow-faced youths who knew nothing about killing or being killed, whose virginal bodies were dressed to look like soldiers, and whose hands clung nervously to the rifle, knowing that when Jerry appeared they had to ease back the trigger and fight for their lives. They no more wanted to kill than anyone else, and yet they had no option. It was, Henry had found out himself, kill or be killed. When he spoke about those terrible years and the awful battle of the Somme, his blue eyes would fill with tears. I could see that behind them there was an enormous waterfall of emotion that occasionally over-spilled and dropped salt tears down his cheek. Sometimes I would touch them with my finger, sometimes I would hold his head to my chest and gently lick his salty wounds.

He was, as I have tried to express, a wonderful part of my life, and so separated from everything else that was happening during that time. I still think about him very deeply, and I remember with fondness the beautiful love letters that spilled out of his soul day after day. He was a gentle, understanding man who knew a woman's fears and who never took more than was offered. Even after our relationship drifted into calmer waters ('terminated willy-nilly' he wrote in a letter to me dated 'Polling Day') we continued to correspond. Very often his outpourings would cover pages and pages, and a great flat envelope would plop through my letterbox filled with a long letter, some pages of manuscript, and the rose petals which used to accompany every letter he sent to me. What wonderful letters he would write! They spoke to me just as if he were lying by my side. They brought back our conversations so vividly.

He would prop his chin up with his hand, and talk – at first gently, and then with growing speed and exclamation, almost as if he were living the book he was writing at the time.

'I say again and again to myself, expect nothing, you ex-starborn fool, don't build up, STOP your imagination from eating your life away, or rather, employ it in creating something new. I have cut short the series [the *Chronicle of Ancient Sunlight*] and ended it with number fourteen,[4] that composite of more than a dozen ragged and partly lost versions, because it seemed best to stop at October 1945; though it will leave the fate of a few characters in the air: such as Richard Maddison, Phillip's two sisters whom he dislikes, and Melissa, last heard of in the Far East as the Japs are creeping down the Malay Peninsula to Singapore, and on the way holding bayonet practices on British soldiers lying on the ground with hands tied behind them, while people look on. A terrible scene in my book, as this news comes over the BBC in December 1941, with the *Repulse* and the *Prince of Wales*, two battleships, sunk by the Japs' bombing because we had no air cover there, no aircraft carrier. A "Mrs Valiant" worked in my farmhouse kitchen, and she had a son, Mark, who was a Norfolk territorial and was sent out to Singapore two weeks before the fall of that "impregnable" fortress. (It was, from the sea; but the Japs sneaked down the forests from behind, after our two great capital ships were simply sunk by bomb after bomb. It was the low point of the war for us; one defeat and seeming ruin after another.)

'Mrs Valiant wept in the kitchen; everyone had gone to her in the village to say, "Oh, your poor Mark, taken prisoner and bayoneted", until she wept silently as she washed up. I, the traitor and outcast,[5] told her it was only propaganda. I hugged her, she wept on my shoulder, I said all would come right, it was put out by the BBC to make us mad and stir us up. She said next day that she had kept her sanity that night by repeating the words I had said, while I wished I had been at Singapore instead of rotting in a corner of England, fighting the war in my mind, trying to think what I could do to stop it before the country, Empire, and Europe went down into eternal night, a lost civilization.

'Well this is all now told by Phillip, who has taken over my straight and factual autobiography, with additions I could not or did not include, but only hint at, at the end, when the purge has come and in the hour of his apparent defeat and disgrace and imminent ruin – family gone, farm animals wandering about unattended, War Ag. Committee about to take over the land and possess it – they could have done that, and did with some inefficient farms: just cancel the title deeds and out goes the old owner, and quite right too in wartime, with townees having one egg a month on ration, two ounces of butter a week, and a scrap of meat or bones.'

Henry would have to change his position by this time; he would be getting stiff. But nothing was allowed to interrupt his flow once he began talking about the book.

'*Eh bien*, Phillip finds all gone on the farm; Billy his son is estranged because of Phillip's treatment of his step-mother Lucy; Lucy has broken down and gone away weeping, with the small children, to an undisclosed destination; and Phillip returns from South Devon and his blown-up *Gartenfeste* which had been taken over, and all civilians in the area sent away, for a battle practice with live shells and bullets, in preparation for D-Day. Phillip's trees are destroyed by shellfire. He finds an empty farmhouse, with Peter, removed from school before his time, in charge.

'Phillip has drained and ploughed the eighty acres of low-lying meadows, but the corn on them has been water-slain by exceptional floods in the winter; the meadows lie behind a sea-wall, with a one-way sluice which the press of tides behind the sea-wall keeps shut until the salt water ebbs, then the water-pressure pushes the sluice open. Meanwhile, the river flood-water spreads all over the meadows . . .'

Henry's brow would pucker with the anxiety he felt for his characters. Relentlessly he would continue talking.

'Wheat rotten and dead in swamps; pigs no good; tractor-bearing gone; Eyeties lousy (Italian prisoners who lie about all day in gangs and do no work except to snare and cook small birds); milking plant lost; foreman n.b.g.

'Phillip, wandering aimless and broken at last, sees the lorry, painted dark green, covered with strange satirical figures and sketches. Is that wild angular figure, with waving arms, chasing away soldiers, me? And the scarecrow chained to a little grey donkey a self-portrait of Peter, who has scrawled these words?

'Before this, Phillip thinks of his eldest son Billy, who ran away to join the RAF. "If only I'd been less dictatorial, less tense, Billy would still be here."

'(Phillip is back from Devon, where he has bought a two-ton milking machine as a last hope to save the farm, which is now in the red. Known locally as the Bad Lands, being steep, hard to plough and cultivate, rains taking down the top fertile soil, no ordinary farmer would ever think of farming such land; but in wartime corn crops were compulsory, and by 1945 P's land is exhausted, its fertility gone.)

'Phillip reflects: "If only I had been . . . less tense, Billy would still be here, he would have stayed the course. A mere colt was entered for the Grand National, against all the rules of horsemanship, and after the worst of trainings. Since the age of fourteen, when the war began and I took him away from school, this boy whose face I am always seeing before me, fixed as it were to the petrification of the heart, this child with greenish-grey face looking as though paraffin were in his blood-stream, his movement languid in thick dark clothing covered by oil-stained overalls which he wore throughout the year, sleeves never rolled up even during the hottest harvest sun; no boyhood, all work and no play, jobs always behindhand, implements broken and no one to repair them, tail-boards of trailers being backed, splintered, against hedgebanks and walls, tractor spud-wheels going over ladders left in the grass, front wheels falling off because roller-bearings were worn and when they were replaced by another set the engine broke; so that all went on slower and slower, until he felt like a fly on flypaper, and all the dead flies on the flypaper were the hundreds of things that were never done properly, and worst of all he knew he was not doing them properly, and felt as a fly feels trying hard to walk on sticky flypaper. All Saturday and Sunday Billy had to sit on the Little Grey Donkey and be laughed at for it, for the village lads down by the bridge had never heard of anyone else having a Fergusson tractor, and the village was the entire world to Billy. And Dad mobbed and mobbed him until he hardly knew what he was doing; he was bound to be mobbed anyway, so in the end it didn't matter what he said or did, and now he is dead."

'Phillip is sitting by a hedge, "with everything to do and nothing left to do it with"; i.e., he is broken down, listening to goldfinches at the August thistle-seed, twittering happily as they "cross the air", while Phillip thinks of all the years he did not stop to listen to them . . .

'The narrative continues. Now it is time to return to the farmhouse to see Mrs Valiant, who has been coming every day to prepare meals – out of one meagre weekly ration – for the child whom she insists on calling Master Peter. Mrs Valiant is not well; her legs are painful, and she is slow; but she could not, she says, leave Master Peter alone. Mrs Valiant has learned, by telegram from the Secretary of State for War, that her own boy, Luke, died on the Burma railway more than two years before. Her eyes are bright with unfallen tears as she says to me: "My boy should have stopped here where he belongs, sir, and helped Master Billy on the farm."

'I sit in the granary, and wander about the loft, where the old sporting prints are still in their pre-war newspaper-wrappings in the tea-chests we brought up from Dorset; and for a moment it seems, as on one or two occasions during the past eight years, that there is only one way to avoid a charge in the courts that might wreck the career of a writer who is also the family provider – unless the charge be defended, which is unthinkable.

'But *la balance, toujours la balance*, as Philippe Pétain was constantly saying to himself during the German occupation. He did not run away, and return and fight another day; he stood; and the mob has dishonoured him. Stripped of rank, honours, and decorations as a Marshal of France, this old soldier, "the saviour of Verdun" in 1916, lies in solitary confinement awaiting trial, not by his peers, as a traitor. Let him not defend himself. "Good night, sweet Prince, And flights of angels sing thee to thy rest."

'And lots more on the same theme, a unique record of a European unit who saw both sides at once, and a person who saw the faults of both sides in himself. Maybe the reader will see the virtues too. But Phillip is doomed; he was doomed as the donkey boy;[6] he died in the first war, rose again as a phoenix. A dove-like girl, Melissa, Lucy's cousin, loved him, but he was held away from her by a greater love, although he did not know this at the time, deeming it his infirmity.'

To me, his listener, it seemed almost unnatural that Henry did not even pause for a drink. He was a fine talker, however, to me absolutely fascinating, and on he would press with what he felt he must say.

'So maybe it would be artistically better to leave Phillip at the end of this ultimate chapter? The village black-marketeer, Mr Harcourt Bugg – who has collected gold sovereigns during the war, paying £6 each – who informs against Phillip to the police in 1940 as a "self-confessed Hitler agent, paid six quid a week by Hitler", in September 1945 gets his hoard of sovereigns smuggled to France – via RAF plane at Cambridge – where he gets £8 each for them: the same Harcourt Bugg tells Phillip when the farm is sold that he isn't the only one to make money out of the war (referring to his sale of the farm to Phillip). But then he shows Phillip his rolls of pound notes, proudly, and tells him about the smuggling of gold abroad. This patriot!

'Then follows Phillip recalling, but to himself, some dis-graceful items from the papers: such as (true) an ex-Sports-writer of a daily paper, now a Tank Major DSO, MC, writing that he over-ran German boys of nine and ten years old who were throwing stones at his tank: "thus to help exterminate the evil inherent in a race which", etc., etc.

'Harcourt Bugg asks: "So you've read about it, have you?"

' "Yes, I read about it."

' "That's us," says Bugg proudly, "that's the clique I'm with. What about your pal Birkin[7] now, eh?"

' "He's very ill."

' "He went too far; he was a good man before he left the Conservatives. Why he ever joined up with the Socialists I can't think; he was a rich man, why didn't he look after his money?"

' "How do you know I won't tell the police about your gold smuggling?"

' "I know you're not the man to do a thing like that," Bugg replies; which makes me smile for his innocence.

'So the wheel comes round again, and Phillip understands all, so can condemn nothing in others; only in himself. He has all the gifts which will ruin any man. He has love in his heart, he sees Hitler as one caught up in the gale of the world,[8] which destroyed him and all his works. He will make a trust of his sale of the farm, all for the family, together with his copyrights, and return, as he started in 1921, to South Devon and try to begin again. Alone. And so everything in his life has the same pattern, the same results.

'And now it is all done. Thought of in 1919, attempted in 1929, smouldered within, at times painfully for the frustration, until 1949, when, for the tremulously afraid, haunted author, it is over. The flowers have been pollinated, the seeds formed, the plant has had its time. Praise be.

'And the author does not know where to go, or stay, what to do. Those words, by the way, I quoted for Pétain – who was stripped and died in prison, alone, although he had a wife – are from the end of *Hamlet*, when Hamlet is run through by a sword after he has run through his usurping uncle.

' "Now cracks a noble heart. Good night, sweet Prince, And flights of angels sing thee to thy rest!"

'And just at the end someone says – and this applies to all history of men upon this earth –

> Now let me speak to the yet unknowing world
> How these things came about: so shall you hear
> Of carnal bloody and unnatural acts,
> Of accidental judgements, casual slaughters,
> Of deaths put on by cunning and forc'd cause,
> And, in this upshot, purposes mistook
> Fallen on the inventors' heads: all this can I
> Truly deliver.

'Which might be the theme of *A Chronicle of Ancient Sunlight* . . .'

Abruptly the theme would change. Some connection, unknown to me, would be made in Henry's mind, and he would start muttering, gradually becoming his eloquent self.

'I have stomach cramps, a joint most painful in the hip of one of my eight legs – I am Arachne, the spinning spider – and headache. I hope I'll be well enough to motor to Broxford tomorrow. I wanted to cut the overgrown and misery-making sight of thorn hedge in field today, but an early rain said: "Ah, you *can't* now, you see"; and so here I am, settled down, a man muttering to himself, a dotard and misfit and generally finished product . . .

'You know I was *lent* that 1100cc car. It is wonderful to steer, the engine pulls it round corners by the front wheels, so you never turn over unless you can't turn the wheel at speed. It isn't made in an estate body unfortunately, so I shan't buy it. I've looked at a Ford Cortina, also a Triumph Herald which is very good. But rear seats have only wee room for passengers' legs, about five inches; not good, as the front seats bear on the knees. Otherwise lovely, 70 mph in third gear, which will pass any lumbering old trash belching smoke on the road. So I'll be in the old HOD, for which I am allowed £300 part exchange *if* it is in the same condition when I return on Wednesday morning. By then it will have done 50,000 miles, which is a lot; but the engine is fine and good . . .

'I think I see a key in what you say about your mum; you love her much but can't or don't show it. Don't worry about that. You are not frozen or psychocrattered cluttered-up at all. You have an unusual mind in that you think with your head, and not as I do often and fatally with the feelings. That is good, to use your head, it is the classic type of mind. As for your frozen feelings, when your true prince comes along the sleeping beauty will awake. I have thought I have seen signs of a vernal uprising in you. You are like a wild fox, not like a cat whose ancestors for ages have been domesticated and so have lost the natural wild fear of Man. A young tame fox hasn't. It is as sharp as its needle teeth. But it will yield and play with and trust the one who has brought it up, and will never forget that human guardian for the love it was given. Melissa was like that: a one-man girl. Scores were after the original of this character, everyone loved her, she was beautiful, poised, and full of fun, and had a very direct, to me scaring, mind. She said once: "Your quality has put to shade all the young men who seem to like me, even to want me. And you don't want me, do you?"

'This was a tremendous thing for the young girl to say. She was pale, she wasn't very well as a child, even at 21 she had to be fed on glucose as she lost energy very quickly since she burned her power in intense feeling. I was just a wee bit scared of her, partly because of her family, which was large and extensive and one of the historic families of England; while I was a nobody, and felt it acutely at times, for the talent which was recognized was nothing to me; indeed, I felt a fraud.

'This was due, I know, to coming from an unhappy home; it was nothing really to do with money or "position", but came from a lack of harmony between parents in the early years. It can, and does, happen in one particular moment: the child is *stricken*. Like a lightning flash: scorched. In years to come it is *odd*. Can't love. Idealises excessively. Its nature is cramped within. Only love can bring forth, in time, the blossoming of the personality. That's why Jesus, who could "heal the sick" – give them heart and hope – said that God is love. Love is one of the great creative forces of this brute world: therein lies all hope, all faith, all confidence. And when one comes through to this love one is changed, reborn, a new person. The outlook lights up, in the mind anyway. The ancient term of the Greek mysteries, long before Jesus was born of woman, was parthenogenesis. Partheno, maiden – genesis, birth. Virgin birth. This as translated into English became "conception without spermatozoa"; i.e., male sperm which conjoins with the female egg to produce a dear little foxy, or even a nasty little old donkey boy.

'You are still the sleeping princess; tenderness and companionship, when you find it, will do the rest.'

Here, Henry's mind would again shift key; another

theme emerges; to him a continuation of the logic of his thoughts. His voice, as always, became stronger.

'I should be hoovering the rooms; cutting those six-inch-thick beech dwarfs in my hedge. Cut to the stub, six inches off the ground, they will then sprout, and I'll keep the hedge two feet six inches high every year; else they rush up and take all the topsoil nourishment of the veg. garden. Parsnips: those bloody sheep ate the tops but didn't dig like badgers for the roots. I did so want wallflowers to bloom this spring, so that anyone coming – well, you – would see blossoms. Now I am desolate, the field is bare, and oh so much work is required; and here I sit and dream all day, with about 75 per cent nightmare, or dull frightened thoughts. It may be irritating to have too many bods in a house, but it doesn't gnaw like loneliness and fear. However, *Labor omnia vincit*, which means work occupies the mind and conquers all the mists and vapours of idleness. . . .

'I had *three* telephone calls on Saturday. Usually I have only about one a week. One was from a friend, aunt of Melissa, asking me to a party on Sunday at 6 for a drink with neighbours, near Barnstaple, and to stay to supper with her afterwards. The next was from a motoring friend offering me the Morris 1100cc for weekend. So I went on to tea at Instow with the mother of Melissa. Then to see E. W. Martin, who is to speak on 14 May.[9] Then down to the Fox and Hounds to see my old pal the Brigadier. Three pints of ale, and back to Ernie Martin at Black Torrington where I'd left my tobacco. Home at 10.15 p.m. to eat my oven-cooked timer-clock casserole and listen to "Not so Much a Muckup as a Weighing Up of Slife". My *third* call on Saturday was from a German, who said he was flying to New York on Friday next, so couldn't dine with me at The Odd Volumes[10] – limited to fifty members – at the Savage Club. He wants to meet me as I have stuck up for his grandfather the Kaiser, who never said "Walk over the contemptible little British Army" (in 1914). But we shall, he hopes, meet in London later on. He is Prince Frederick of Prussia, whose son is now a private in the British Army . . .

' "Dear Ophelia, I am sick of these numbers. But thou

would'st not know how ill's all here about my heart." '

On odd occasions we would row; not intensely, we would just disagree about something. I suppose, to be perfectly honest, I enjoyed the luxury of his friendship. He introduced me to quite a few literary people and to members of his family, one of whom was Julian Bream, who was at that time married to one of Henry's daughters. He was a man completely absorbed in his work, as was Henry.

One of Henry's sons lived on a nature reserve somewhere in Sussex. I remember that Henry and I once went down there for the weekend. He was unlike Henry in appearance, but had something of Henry's manner. He was a warden for the Nature Conservancy Council, and the cottage where he and his wife lived was typical of their lifestyle. He was dedicated to the preservation of the countryside. His wife had just had a baby, and they had named the child after a wild bird. It was one of those special weekends; the kind one always remembers. I experienced such happiness walking on the Downs with Henry, listening as he imitated the birds; and, in the evening, lying in his arms while the log fire crackled, hearing him read a chapter from his latest book.

If only the timing had been right things might have been different. I did truly love him; I still do.

Dear Henry, he was so brilliant. If only one could have studied his brain and made a blueprint of it, one would have had the perfect formula for a human being. He was in every conceivable respect one of the most understanding and endearing men I have known. Eccentric he was; a hermit, of course, but at times a gregarious one. Henry Williamson was a man desperate for love, bubbling with his chronicles of life. It does seem ironic that one who had said so much still trod a solitary stretch across the lonely plains of life in search of his Lucifer.

His familiar name for me was Foxy. He would sit stroking my hair and reliving the beautiful moments he had spent with his own dear cherished foxy friend he had saved from the hunters. I responded to the name, feeling that I was indeed a fox to him.

Henry often talked about the recent and shattering affair he had had with a woman writer, and from which he had now recovered. When she was staying with him she had called him her Prospero, and his hut was their kingdom. Apparently she had looked after him for three or four weeks, but had had to leave because she found that he was too absorbing, so that she could not concentrate on her own work. At that time he was writing *The Phoenix Generation*,[11] and had been particularly moved by the chapter he had just completed, in which Phillip and Melissa each recall the incident, recounted in *A Test to Destruction*,[11] when Phillip, who had been blinded, takes the bandages off his eyes and sees before him Melissa, then a beautiful child, and talks to her.

When he read from a newly-typed piece of his own work I could always visualize the countryside he was describing. In a strange sort of way, this gentle warrior seemed to have mastered nature and taken it into his grasp. He knew the ways of the bullfrog, the birds of the trees, and the fish in the streams. He knew the sky and the very earth on which he trod. As he read slowly through numerous pages, I saw him as a kind of Omar Khayyam: perhaps my own guru, a magical figure who knew the ways of God. We had often talked about religion, and Henry called Jesus the greatest hero of our times. Phillip Maddison was Henry of course. In the *Chronicle* the story was of a man's love and hate of the world. Phillip had loved one woman in his life – Lucy, his wife – and when she died giving birth to their child he tried to remarry time and time again.

In one of our sessions Henry stopped reading for a while, and looked at me. 'Here', he said, 'is a letter that was written to me when I was in the army. It was from a priest who was later killed in the front lines. He was another great man, and certainly one who knew me both inwardly and outwardly. This priest would go with the men up to the front line, dressed in his priest's clothes, and he would comfort those who were afraid, or talk tenderly to the shocked and dying; and one day he just didn't come back.'[12] Henry bowed his head, and a tear fell. He tried to hide his sorrow, but I could feel it flickering in his eyes. I held his head, as I had done so many times, and gently stroked the soft hair on his head. He pressed his lips against my neck, and took me in his arms. I must have aroused great passions in him; yet his body, browned by the summer sun and godlike in its beauty, made me want only to lie next to him, and be a part of his own sweet sunlight.

In bed we were as one, entwined as though nothing on this earth could ever change our fate. Ours was a wonderful love; an extreme sense of peace reigned over me during that time. His hands gentled my turbulent flesh, while his lips kissed away the problems of the day, and I felt a tenderness which burst from within him. I adored and cherished every moment with him. He would soothe me to sleep, holding me in his arms all night lest I ran away like his beautiful Tarka. He would love and guide me through stormy emotional waters. I have never known such love in my life. It was complete and fulfilling, and I think if I live to be one hundred I shall never find such richness in a man again. 'Truth and love will I bear unto thee,' he used to say, his sad eyes staring up at me, his face etched in my mind, and the beauty of his mind inspiring in me hopes that I too might become a writer.

I can never forget him. He is to me as immortal as the ancient sunlight in the sky. He is as true as Mother Nature herself; perhaps in another time and another space I could live at peace with myself, if only I could recapture those beautiful years.

Alicante, Spain, 1986

NOTES

1. *The Star-Born*, a 'Celestial Fantasy', 'with an introduction by Henry Williamson', the authorship being attributed to Williamson's fictional character Willie Maddison. First edition, with illustrations by C. F. Tunnicliffe, 1933. Revised edition, illustrated by Mildred E. Eldridge, 1948.

2. *Tarka the Otter*, 1927, still Henry Williamson's most famous book, was to have been filmed by Walt Disney, but Williamson vetoed the proposal. *Tarka* was eventually filmed in England in 1977; the filming being completed on the day of Henry's death.

3. *The Dream of Fair Women*: a tale of youth after the Great War, 1924. Revised edition, 1931. This is the third novel in Williamson's tetralogy *The Flax of Dream*, the first two being *The Beautiful Years* and *Dandelion Days* (1921 and 1922; revised editions 1929 and 1930). The *Flax of Dream* series, concluded in *The Pathway* (1928 and 1931) has seldom been out of print for long.

4. *A Chronicle of Ancient Sunlight*: this novel-series, begun in 1949 and completed in 1967, was finally achieved in fifteen volumes; the first, *The Dark Lantern*, was published in 1951, the last, *The Gale of the World*, in 1969.

5. During the Second World War Henry Williamson endured much hostility from some of his neighbours on account of his pre-war support for the policies of Sir Oswald Mosley, who opposed the idea of a second war with Germany. Williamson has written of these troubles in his autobiographical book *The Story of a Norfolk Farm* (1941) and in his novel *The Phasian Bird* (1948), as well as in the final volumes of the *Chronicle*.

6. In the second volume of the *Chronicle*, the life of Richard and Hetty Maddison's baby son Phillip is saved when an old man, a veteran of Waterloo, advises Phillip's parents to give the ailing infant ass's milk to drink.

7. Sir Hereward Birkin, under which name Sir Oswald Mosley appears in *A Solitary War* and *Lucifer Before Sunrise*, the thirteenth and fourteenth volumes of the *Chronicle*.

8. Before his murder, by the supporters of Josef Brodz, alias Tito, the Jugoslav patriotic leader General Mihaelovitch declared that he had been caught up in the gale of the world.

34

9. Ernest Martin, historian and sociologist. He, Ted Hughes, and Brocard Sewell, were the three invited speakers at the formal presentation by Henry Williamson of all his pre-1949 manuscripts to the University of Exeter, on 14 May 1965. The manuscripts were valued then at £50,000. This act of generosity was not reciprocated by the University. Two attempts, supported by two successive Vice-Chancellors, to obtain for Williamson an honorary doctorate were vetoed by a majority vote of the Degrees Committee of the University.

10. The Sette of Odde Volumes: a private dining club for bibliophiles. It is a considerable honour to be elected a member.

11. *The Phoenix Generation*: volume twelve of *A Chronicle of Ancient Sunlight. A Text to Destruction*, ibid., volume six.

12. Father Aloysius in *A Chronicle of Ancient Sunlight* appears to be modelled on this priest. Williamson had intended to give a broadcast talk on the 'real' Father Aloysius, but never did so, and his identity remains unknown.

This book
has been published by
The Aylesford Press
158 Moreton Road, Upton, Wirral, Cheshire.

Set in 12-point Monotype Baskerville
and printed and bound by
Smith Settle, Ilkley Road, Otley, West Yorkshire
in a limited edition of 460 copies
on Antique Laid paper.

400 copies are bound in paper covers.

60 copies, of which 50 are for sale,
are bound in quarter goatskin
and signed by the authors.

This is copy number

118